Inner Warfare

a memoir

Anissa Fritz

publishing house

First Edition: February 2017

ISBN 13: 978-0692850916

Published by: Thirty West Publishing House

www.thirtywestph.com

Cover design: Jessica C. Barros

www.jessicacbarrosart.com

Printed in: United States of America

AUTHOR'S NOTE

Although in-depth descriptions of my blood, sweat, and tears fill this book, it is important to note the hard-work, perseverance, and love of those who were consistently behind the scenes of this project.

I would like to first off thank Thirty West Publishing House for helping me transform my ashes into beauty. From editing to designing, to promoting, the efforts and support of the team at Thirty West

is what gives this book shape. Especially Jessica C. Barros, the in-house artist at Thirty West and one of the very few people I truly admire. When my demons said I couldn't, she said I could. And therefore, I did. She gave me back the wings I forgot I had.

Hannah, Chessa, Skylar, my roommates and best friends who saw me write the majority of this novel through sleepless nights, anxiety attacks, tears, and doubt: my words would not be on these pages without each of you. Each page contains tints of Hannah's bravery, Chessa's compassion, and Skylar's intelligence, all traits that make them the admirable humans that I am ridiculously blessed to call my lifelong friends.

Michael and Cynthia, my parents. They gave me life, and unconditionally loved me even when I wanted to take that life away. I saw worthless; they saw priceless. I never idolized models or actors now or even in my youth. That is because from age five to age one hundred and five; I will stand firm in knowing that the two people who lived life right were them.

This book is not meant to shame, guilt, hurt, or condemn. It is not meant for pity or attention. This book was created for those who feel lost, damned, damaged, frayed, or alone.

You are not alone. You are not damaged goods, and you are not a hopeless cause.

You are unbroken.

For those who choose to wage war against their demons. For those whose days are filled with battle cries and whose nights are tormented with restlessness. To the warriors, soldiers, and champions of their inner warfare. This is for you.

Inner Warfare

1

Blood. The bathtub was no longer a vessel of hot water, but rather a lukewarm pool of light red with a razor sitting at its floor like a sunken treasure. My naked body slumped like an overused rag doll. One arm submerged in the wine-like liquid that rose to my belly button, the other hung over the tub's cream porcelain edge. Drops of blood trickled from horizontal slits on my wrist, down my newly manicured fingertip, and finally kissed the white tile floor.

One drop.

I'm six in my grandparents' backyard. It was summer in Texas, but by some miracle, there was a cool breeze. My cousin Aaron bested me in age, size, and athletic skill. Despite these facts, life hadn't dealt my six-year-old soul any bad hands yet, and my competitive nature was in full uproar. When a touch football game between the uncles and older cousins came to life, I jumped in like an ill-equipped, untrained soldier whose biggest downfall would be an excess of confidence. It didn't take long until I found myself face down in the grass with my uncle profusely apologizing for playing too roughly. I stood up quickly, ready to prove that I was still tough enough to play with the boys. That was when my mouth tasted it - Metal. It was salty and thick. It was blood. A stream of it ran from my cheek where the ground had torn at my skin and trickled into my mouth.

The tough-girl charade was up; I cried. The tears were as hot as they were plenty, and hiccups from lack of oxygen frequently interrupted my wailing. It wasn't the pain that caused the tears. It was the blood. It registered as a sign that my body was currently tainted and would begin to undergo a healing process. Fifteen years later, an exclamation-point-shaped scar on my left cheek is the result.

More red drops.

It was at this moment that I was no longer scared of blood but embraced it to the point where I could draw it out of my skin with the calculated swipe of a blade.

Another drop.

The first time was a drunken accident. Blurred vision, lack of balance, and a brand new shaving razor resulted in a small, jagged nick on my left wrist. I don't remember what I drank that night. I don't remember what I wore. I don't remember the names of the drinks I drank or the names of the boys who bought them. Instead, the memory of a red line appearing on my skin is ingrained in my brain.

Funny how we unintentionally choose to remember some things and not others, isn't it?

The blood ran free. The blood was consistent. Even after water washed it away, another red line came to life again. I envied it.

Two simultaneous drops.

My eyes drooped, and my body sagged further. I was up to my rib cage in wine now. My mind ran away from the porcelain tub and dumped me on a tile floor that was just as cold as the florescent lights were unforgiving.

The sound of beeps, dings and humming medical machinery came together as one to form my favorite childhood song: the sound of my mother living.

Eight years old and that is when I second handily faced death. It hung over my mother as a brand new scar tore down her chest like a fashion statement. That day, and every day after, I knew the pink, jagged mark as a survivor's statement. The scar ran down her chest, a tube ran down her throat, an I.V. ran down her arm, and a tear ran down my face. Before then, having something taken away from me meant no dessert because I wouldn't eat my broccoli. Now death loomed over my mom, and all I could do was sit on the cold tile because my young limbs were too gangly and uncoordinated to weave through the maze of wires that had now become my mother's lifelines.

Another drop.

Death didn't scare me now.

I don't remember the knocks on the door or any other sign of warning that Hannah was coming in. The image of Hannah - my best friend, my roommate - standing in my bathroom doorway looking down at the destruction I had caused will never fail to escape me, no matter how many pills I take.

The tile is a mess; the only thought I could muster, much less any audible words.

Hannah went into autopilot. They say practice makes perfect, and I gave her plenty of practice. She had cleaned up my self-induced blood from her bedroom carpet, the walls of our apartment, and my white tiled bathroom several times over the last three months. In fact, it was only four hours earlier that she perfectly bandaged my forearm to now see her work destroyed and reopened with new additions.

Open the laundry doors. Grab the medicine box. Get the gauze and the medicine tape.

Hannah moved like clockwork. I lay there useless but mystified. In these moments, she wasn't an equal but a superior.

Guilt swallowed me whenever I made her do this.

Please don't be mad at me, please don't hate me, and please don't leave me.

Guilt was the head conductor on my train of guilty thought, and I was a first-class passenger.

Not a crease of stress ran across Hannah's face, and not a strand of her dark hair seemed to move out of place from her purposely messy bun. She was stoic but concentrated, as if she had just spilled nail polish and had to wipe it up before it dried. Her composure held firm until she hit the floor. That's when Hannah's tough-girl charade ended.

I'm not sure what it is about white tile, but I think it breaks even the strongest of life's soldiers. When Hannah's knees met those square pieces of bathroom flooring she, too, broke. Her brokenness didn't come in the form of blood drops and a razor with microscopic pieces of skin lodged in between the blades. Her brokenness came in the form of a teardrop that fell onto the white gauze that she meticulously wrapped around my left wrist for what seemed like the hundredth time. With each angelic teardrop that fell from her heaven eyes arose a demonic red drop of blood from the hell that was once enclosed by my now open skin.

"Anissa, I think it's time we go to the hospital," she said.

I wouldn't know that she had spoken these words until weeks later when she repeated them as we recounted that night over pitchers of cheap beer at a bar near our college campus. Pitchers of lukewarm alcohol that I often purchased as one of my numerously feeble and inadequate ways of thanking her for saving my life.

"You need help," she said as she moved to my right arm.

This time, her words registered. My eyes gazed at the abstract shapes of red that seeped through the white gauze that now tightly hugged both of my forearms. My gaze momentarily shifted to her watery, scared eyes, then back to my arms.

Why am I like this?

"Okay," I said.

Things went dark after that.

2

The "Emergency Room" sign blared bright and red at 1 a.m. The mirroring between the red of myself inflicted wounds and the red neon lights that marked the place of healing those wounds still makes me laugh internally. Funny how the same place that I had first seen death and feared it was now the place that I was taken to when my fear had turned into dispassion for life. Except it was no longer my mother's life that was waging war with death. It was my own, and I wasn't equipped to put up a fight.

3

Being depressed isn't as obvious as pushing out the back panel from the locked gun closet in your grandfather's basement and placing an unloaded Glock 3 in your mouth just to feel the barrel on your tongue.

It can be on your drive home from work.

Amid your autopilot commute, you wonder what it would feel like to jerk your steering wheel as far to the right as you can.

You adjust your grip on the European engineering.

Would your car spin out of control? Would it happen in slow motion like the movies? Would your car wrap around a pole? Would you hurt someone else? Would you be injured? Would you die?

Before you force yourself to think of something else, you question your sanity.

Why?

Because you veered to the right when the thought of death danced in your brain, just for a split second. Not enough to cause an accident. Not even enough to get the teenager riding your bumper to look up from his phone. Just enough for you to notice the thought transference to reality. A slight action, carrying deadly meaning.

You change your grip on the wheel and wonder what you're going to eat for dinner.

4

Depression can be on the backburner of your mind at a constant simmer for years. It can be front and center, boiling over to your immediate thought at all hours of the day. It can retreat and lay off on days you would expect it to destroy you. It can bang on the front door of your psyche when you specifically did not invite guests that could ruin your scheduled night of fun.

The concoction of depression that the demons choose was handpicked for you. This personally crafted gift from the monsters under your bed have no rules, no mercy, and no limitations.

5

It's there on rainy days.

It's there when the rain drops hit your bedroom window to create a chorus of thumps that sound like the anxious fingers of a midnight lover tapping away at the glass. It's there on the interstate of streaks that have been left by raindrops that succumbed to gravity and plummeted to your window sill. The rumble of the sky matches the unrest of your essence. The nudge of a drizzly breeze feels like a lob to the center of your back, leaving you grappling with your lungs to regain the luxury of breathing without effort. A cutting wind howls as it snakes through streets and in between gates, jumps fences, claws at the foot your bedroom door, and becomes the personification of the dark figures swarming your psyche in hopes to seep through an overlooked crack, patiently waiting to consume you. The wind is pawing outside leaks through your barrier of locked doors and blankets.

It infiltrates your room and ploddingly transforms your safe space into a mere four walls that manipulate your knees to bow in compliance to the agonizing cold. The dark figures are hungry, and the rain makes the barriers of your mind soggy and permeable. You let them rampage your spirit with tormenting words, images, and memories.

The torture on your mind begins.

Your fists tighten around the bed sheets in the last ditch attempt at a hold on reality. The abuse triggers a storm of tears to erupt from your clenched eyelids. With the remains of your consciousness, you pray that it doesn't rain tomorrow.

6

It's there when you're alone.

It penetrates your stomach when you try to enjoy the takeout food that you were mentally preparing to devour since the appeal of not cooking dinner presented itself to you at 10 a.m. You stare at it with disgust that soon shifts from the Styrofoam box of Chinese food onto yourself.

It hacks at your laughter as you lie in bed watching a movie that was created solely to enable the large portion of society who watch movies as a tacky attempt at escaping their mundane lives. As it interrupts your laughter - caused by dingy, overused punchlines - you are forced to recognize that you have become a member of this group in society whom you routinely mocked. You are sucker punched into the realization that you too are attempting to escape, and that you too are failing gloriously. You feel confused and aware: confused as to what you are trying to escape, but aware that regardless of what you're running from, you're not running fast enough.

It trickles through your ears and contorts into grimacing characters that haunted your younger self. It barges in on your dreams and jolts you from sleep via a fit of breathlessness and choking for oxygen. Opposite of alarm clocks, the brain can't be turned off with the click of a button which leaves you making violently unsuccessful attempts to regain sleep for the few precious hours that remain. Each smack of the pillow and frustrated pull of the sheets condemns you to realize that the battle is already lost before the day has begun.

It seeps into you by way of fingertips as your nails run through the surface of your shampoo-soaked scalp. The steam from the hot water creates a foggy haze of atmosphere that matches the interior of your muddled psyche all too well. The pristine of the white tiled walls and porcelain tub seem too clean.

The white would look better with a hint of red, wouldn't it?

The vulnerability of bare skin and wet hair makes you easy prey.

I really am worthless, aren't I?

The accessibility of razor sharp blades being only an arm's length away makes it an easy task.

It wouldn't even hurt that bad, right?

The demons begin to personify; they've come out to play.

It's there when you're surrounded.

It's there when you're having drinks downtown with your friends on a Saturday night. It's there when you're buried under the aftermath of wrapping paper from the presents that were mauled by your family's anxious hands on Christmas morning. It's there when you're at birthday parties, even your own.

It finds you within the sardine can of a bar. The laughter of your friends, the clanking of the glass against glass, and the upbeat music all somehow become both deafening and muffled. Without warning, you now feel as though you are watching your friends from a distance. The crowded club you are in has now adapted the semblance of a desolate highway gas station at 3 a.m. A drunken girl's shoulder meets with yours in her failed attempt at walking in shoes that are too rigid and resultantly incapable of counterbalancing her lopsided stagger. You're not at a deserted gas station; you're at your favorite nightclub with some of your favorite people.

Feelings of isolation, alienation, and detachment linger in your brain. In a room packed full of people, it manages to make you feel alone. When your friends are in arm's reach of you, it has the power to ingrain your brain with the theory that you are not wanted, that you are not needed. You stray away from the group, go home, and erupt into a frenzied outburst of petulance towards yourself and insecurity towards your placement within your friend group.

Whether you end the night contemplating why you deliberately isolated yourself when the night was on track for success, or you scrutinize the validity and honesty of every personal relationship you've possessed, the evening concludes the same. The night ends with your mind swarming of negative thoughts filled with self-doubt, worthlessness, and abandonment. It intrudes your dreams and persecutes you repeatedly and brutally until the awakening cold sweat that clings to your body grants you permission to convince yourself that you simply just had too much to drink.

It was just an off night; you'll stay out all next Saturday night.

You won't. It won tonight, and it will win the next. It will repeatedly overthrow your thoughts the next night and the night after that. Eventually, you give up on going out to bars.

It smirks at the lack of effort it took in getting you to detach yourself from your connections. It leaves you alone for

It continues to win. You continue to lose. It's not done yet.

8

It's there when you're doing what you love.

The one thing you enjoy doing, the one thing you're good at, or the one enjoyable thing you're good at are no exceptions to its destruction.

It turns the writer into a stuttering adolescent with a sloppy grasp of the English language. Words no longer flow with the ease and power that emerge from the triumph of expressing the innermost thoughts into pages filled with tales of heroic feats, battles lost, underdog triumphs and people deemed as ordinary are made extraordinary. Words no longer flow with the graceful ease and calculated power that once had the ability to transform white sheets of paper into canvases bursting with the extremities of human emotion.

It infiltrates the keyboard, the pen, the pencil, and forces them to a halt. It tears existing pages of the writer's sincere compositions. It confuses the writer's syntax, jumbles words, fuddles ideas, and fogs inspiration. The hands that were once the writer's greatest power have now become shaky and insecure extensions of himself that he no longer recognizes. The expressive cord between the writer's mind and fingertips has been cut, leaving the writer an ordinary character who will never have the chance to become extraordinary through his story.

It turns the athlete into an uncoordinated amateur whose body can't perform the aspirations of the mind. It sucks the energy, the drive, the muscles out of the body until the athlete is left exhausted from losing against herself day after day, practice after practice. Running feels like trudging through mud; biking feels like pedaling through the sand; swimming feels like flopping aimlessly in hopes of not drowning; and dribbling, throwing, catching, kicking or hitting a ball feels as pointless and routinely bland as making your bed every morning only to unmake it every night.

It turns the mother emotionless and morphs her into an alien of the home she created. It turns the father into a distant stranger whose lack of words or lack of presence reveal the excess of hopelessness stained into his pupils. It turns the son into a misunderstood outcast of rage, and it turns the daughter into a scavenger of undying love that she will never find at the expense of looking in all the wrong places.

It mangles the things we do and the things we are. Its pillage and plundering of your life do not end there.

9

It's there when you're in love.

You no longer love yourself. The person you're with doesn't either. Even though this is quite possibly the most unjust act of perjury committed by you against yourself, you are unable to see it as such. You feel like a burden. You feel annoying. You feel ashamed when you break out in fits of anxiety, and your significant other has a front row ticket to the freak show starring you. It makes you mutate your partner into your biggest opponent, sometimes to the extent of labeling them the cause of its presence in your life at all. Your lover continues to love you, and you continue to question why. Your lover perpetually loves you, and you perpetually resist.

However, a lover can only be shoved away so often. A lover can only take the razor from your grasp so many times. A lover can only be left without explanation, apology, or remorse for canceled dates, inappropriate behavior, or neglect for so long. A lover can only do so much, since lovers were not meant to work alone but in teams of two.

You leave your partner. You were convinced a flood of relief would follow the breakup and thereby swallow your demons whole, suffocating them to their death. Instead, you are mobbed by your demons who have grown in number and strength. You cry as the guilt of your failed relationship towers over you, and you vomit at the idea of the unpredictable, uncontrollable, destructive wreckage you have become for the amusement of the joy-eaters who continually feast on your afflictions.

10

It's there when it's not supposed to be.

It has no regard for how much money you make or what job you have. It doesn't care if you're thin, overweight, male or female. It doesn't pay heed to the color of your skin, your religion, or your age. It attacks those who don't deserve the inner torture that it brings. It slaughters lives that don't deserve to be defaced and left with barely any life, like a city victimized by a hurricane's power. It violates dreams that don't deserve to be crushed and futures that don't deserve to be terminated.

It will always select undeserving victims because its devastation is deserved by none.

11

It was there when I climbed in the maroon van.

Three steps towards the van, two steps up into the van, and one bend of the knees placed me in my seat. I didn't have to pick a seat because there was only one. The rest of the van, other than the two front seats, housed a cage of black metal with three locks on the right side. The cage enclosed the one seat: mine. The driver's assistant slammed the van door that I had just climbed through but not before locking me inside.

Realistically, it might have been thirty seconds, but in my drug induced, exhausted, hazy state of mind it seemed like thirty minutes at least. That's how I've learned to identify big moments in my life. For some reason, when your life is about to start a new chapter, things seem to slow down.

A cage? Seriously? Where the fuck is my orange jumpsuit?

For some reason, I still had my phone. To this day I don't know if I was allowed to have it or if someone had just slipped on protocol. I unlocked my screen instinctively to text someone but realized I had no idea who I would text. Even if I did have someone to talk to, what was I going to say? A text that read, "Hey sorry I won't be able to go out next Saturday I'm being taken to a mental institution" didn't seem to be the type of thing you're supposed to do when you're given this label; "a danger to oneself" by a medical professional not even eight hours prior.

Eight hours. So much had happened in just eight hours.

12

Hannah's mom, Jen, came to the emergency room at about hour number one.

Jen was something else. She was a spitfire and a professional all wrapped into one, tough-as-nails, single mother. She held my hand a lot that night. While I waited for the nurse to take my vitals, her fingers were wrapped around my lifeless ones. She would squeeze so hard it felt as though she was trying to transfer some of her vitality into my fingertips and up into my brain. Despite her efforts, it didn't work.

Jen made jokes that the male nurse thought I was cute. Without even having to look over, I could feel Hannah rolling her eyes onto the floor at her mom's attempt to make light of the obvious shithole situation. I cracked a smile anyway. Besides, after three months, I was almost as good at faking smiles as I was navigating through hospitals.

After several trips to the bathroom, vital checks, and visits from my male nurse suitor, at about hour three, a social worker sat down by my bed and talked to me about why I was there. At the time, I was hoping she had the answer because I sure as hell didn't.

"Why are you here, Ms. Fritz?"

That was the big, 4 a.m. question.

I remember thinking she looked like a dried up grape. Her hands shook as she began scribbling on her clipboard, and her veins ran above the surface of her skin in blue and green routes that only God himself could keep intact.

A silence lingered in the air. She repeated the question.

"Ms. Fritz, what happened?"

I cried.

She must have been doing this job since before the sun came and crinkled her skin to its current, veiny state. Almost instantaneously she had tissues locked and ready for me.

Through eyes that rained down salty liquid and through several fits of hyperventilation I told her about my demons. I explained that I had been to the doctor five times in the last three months trying new antidepressant after antidepressant after antidepressant until I could no longer take the frustration of my inner demons dodging and defeating any chemical warfare these pills were supposed to wage.

She asked more questions. Nothing I said seemed to throw off her demeanor. That's when I realized that her hands were probably the only shaky aspect about her.

"Do you want to go to a mental institution to get better help?"

I knew the question was going to be asked, but when it was, I froze. It's like knowing for months that you're going to graduate high school and move to college, but when it comes time to part ways with your childhood friends, your heart can't help but feel sad. Some people may call this denial; I just file this feeling under the same category as time slowing down before big life moments.

"Do I even have a real choice?" I asked timidly.

"Well, you could go willingly or unwillingly."

She said it so normally like she was running the drive-thru at McDonald's asking if the customer on the other end of the intercom wanted French fries or apple slices with their kid's meal.

"What's the difference?" I asked, honestly perplexed by what seemed to be a self-explanatory statement.

"If you go willingly, I can send you to a private facility. If you go unwillingly, I have to send you to a state facility."

No, I didn't have a choice.

The choice to get help was taken away as soon as I saw that red, neon emergency room sign above the lobby entrance. It wasn't a question of *if* I wanted to go; it was the question of *where*.

That was the real 4 a.m. question.

I said I would go willingly, and she checked the box on her clipboard that would send me to a private facility to get mental treatment.

Hours four through six, I slept. At least my body slept; my mind didn't. Even in the hospital, my demons continued to mangle the film of what used to be my dreams. Now my brain's late night movies were nothing short of the horror category: butchered fragments of horrific images and dark places. In a facility where people came every day to fend off attacks on their body, I still wasn't safe, not even in my subconscious.

I woke up to too many sounds at once: the sound of the doctor opening the curtains, the sound of my mother crying and whispering "oh my God" over and over, the sound of my dad asking the doctor too many questions all at once such as where I was going and how bad my injuries were, and the sound of the nurse saying the van had arrived. All of these sounds were muffled when Hannah whispered "I love you" in my ear.

At that moment I was grateful that she had drowned out all the other voices with hers, even if it was for just a second. She was the one who broke with me on my bathroom floor eight hours ago: not the doctor, not the nurses, not my parents, but her.

We both knew that this hour would be the last of the "Hannah and Anissa Go to the Hospital" television special.

Those seven hours left a lot of holes in my memory. I can't remember what any of the emergency room staff's names were. I can't remember if I had my phone on me, what Hannah and I talked about, or if I ate. I know I was transferred into a different room at some point in those seven hours, but I don't remember how or when.

I do know that it was at the start of hour one when Jen called my parents, telling them I was in the hospital for cutting my wrists. Within minutes of hanging up the phone, my parents were in the car and on the road ready to embark on the six-and-a-half-hour drive from Texas.

What do you do when the people who gave you life stand over you with tears streaming down their faces as they have just now become aware that the life they gave you isn't a happy one? What do you say when they blame themselves for the cuts on your arms or the demons in your head, but your voice is somehow just as lost as your brain felt when you swiped the blade across your skin?

My mom rushed in like a hurricane, making a beeline for me. She draped herself over me as her tears ran from her cheeks onto my neck, my chest, and even my arms. It was then that I realized the roles had switched. She was now the crying six-year-old who saw death looming over me but could do nothing about it.

Years ago, I had been barricaded out by medical wires and tubes that my uncoordinated limbs were incapable of weaving through. Now I was facing the fried, beaten up, and spat out wires of my brain that had been devoured by depression.

Neither of us was able to help the other.

While my mother's tears drenched my body, I kept my eyes on my dad. As an ex-member of the German Air Force, his stoic disposition didn't leave any room for tears, except for one. I saw one tear run down his cheek. It was the same cheek that I kissed every night before bed after he would read me bedtime stories: the same cheek that was photographed touching mine as we posed like we were dancing at my church's annual Father Daughter Dance. His single tear was the equivalent of my mother's flood.

The first words out of my father's mouth when he saw me are something that not even my inner demons could make me forget.

"Are you okay?"

The words echoed off of the cold hospital flooring and bounced between the three walls that confined me until the question settled into my ear.

Was I okay?

I was in a hospital nightgown with no backside and bandaged from wrist to elbow on both of my arms. My eyes were puffy from crying, and my throat was raw from the tears that turned into frustrated screams. I had been cutting for months and landed myself in an emergency room. I was going to a mental institution to get help: the same type of place that researchers go to make documentaries on severely mentally ill individuals. I couldn't remember the last time I had slept for three hours straight without being awoken by a panic attack or a nightmare. The last time I remember being able to breathe freely was three months ago in Colorado where my feet were strapped to a board, and my mind was free to soar.

Now my mind was a cage that I couldn't escape, and I was trying to cut my soul out of my body in hopes of getting some air. I cut and cut and cut until pools of blood were almost as common as taking a Xanax to relax or a few shots of cheap vodka to numb the pain that was slowly killing me.

If only he knew the half of it.

I could've tried to explain, but, just like everyone else that I had encountered in the last three months, my dad wouldn't understand.

"Yeah, Dad. I'm fine."

14

The slam of the van door brought my train of thought back to the present.

A fucking cage. As if the one in my mind wasn't already doing enough damage, they had to stick me in a physical one to seal the deal. The feeling of emotional entrapment was now met with the physicality of being contained.

The driver's assistant was a man, not old enough for a cane but old enough to have grandkids frolicking somewhere on a farm in Middle of Nowhere, Kansas. He slid into the passenger seat, slammed the passenger side door, and began scribbling on a metal clipboard.

He wore a faded Kansas City Royals baseball cap, and I wondered if he cried last year when the Royals won the World Series after their 30-year drought.

The driver's side door opened and a pudgy woman with a typical mom haircut plopped herself in front of the steering wheel. Her orange hoodie matched her hair except the white roots peeking through the top of her scalp. One hand placed keys in the ignition while the other idly dropped her plastic Big Gulp into the awkwardly-placed cup holder that rested above the A/C vents on the dash.

With my parents following closely behind in their car, the van pulled out of the emergency room roundabout, onto the street, and proceeded en route to the mental facility to which I was assigned.

Neither the orange flare of a driver nor the old Royals fan spoke to me during the 43-minute drive. They did talk to each other, and the pauses in conversation made it clear that they were comfortable in each other's company. They probably had been partners for years, like Goose and Maverick from Top Gun. Instead of flying military planes over war zones, Orange and Royal drove hospital vans containing casualties of mental warfare.

Twenty minutes into the drive, Orange turned into a strip mall parking lot, applying the breaks that let out a squeal of old age, aching for new padding. The van was in park, but neither Royal nor Orange made any motion of getting out of the van.

"Why are we stopping?" I asked, sounding a little more frantic than I intended.

"Your parents got caught behind a train. We're waiting for 'em to catch up," Orange said without even looking over her seatbelt.

What a car ride that must have been. Two parents and a fluffy white dog named Holly that I got in seventh grade following a maroon van that looked, to any other drivers, like any other car in the sea of gas-guzzling vehicles. To Michael and Cynthia Fritz, that maroon van was carrying their only child who was happy, successful, and well-rounded. At least they thought I was.

The illusion of a healthy, happy daughter shattered eight hours ago with an emergency room phone call.

The 43-minute drive following the maroon van filled Michael Fritz's mind with self-loathing, confusion, and tears that he refused to release.

The 43-minute drive following the maroon van would be classified by Cynthia Fritz as terrifying and tear-filled. At minute 40 she would look down at her hands' death grip on the Nissan's leather wheel that had turned her knuckles a ghostly white.

To Holly, the 43-minute drive following the maroon van was just another joyride.

15

A few minutes after the strip mall pit stop, Orange pulled out a pink bedazzled iPhone from her hoodie's front pocket. Her left hand rested on the steering wheel, navigating the road. Her right hand held her phone while her thumb danced across the glass keyboard. Royal's eyes were fixated on the clipboard resting on his lap.

"Fuck. Shannon forgot her lunch. I need to drop it off after this delivery, if that's okay with you," Orange said while shifting her eyes from the road to her cell.

Royal looked up.

"Yeah, no problem. Just make sure to call the next hospital and tell em' we're runnin' late. I take it Joe is too tied up at work to bring it to her?"

A crooked, half-ass smile formed on Royal's face.

The two of them continued to go back and forth, but their voices faded into a goulash of muddled words.

That bitch should not be texting and driving. She probably tells her daughter not to text and drive, and here she is carrying other people's offspring in the cage of her van's backseat while she shifts her eyes from the road to texts filled with typos made from her fat fingers.

I began plotting my lawsuit against her negligence towards my safety. Just because I cut myself didn't give her the right to get me in a car accident possibly. If I wanted to get hurt, it was going to be on my terms, not by the carelessness of this orange monstrosity.

Joe is probably her even-fatter-than-she-is husband who works in an office building. He may even have a cubicle, but that doesn't make up for the fact that his suits are as stale and tasteless as the tuna sandwich that he has eaten for lunch every day for the last 20 years.

Their daughter Shannon is probably the biggest cunt out of the three.

Orange continues to text and steer.

They probably go home and sit down with their TV trays, not caring enough to even sit together at the table, their days too mundane to properly entertain each other over the shitty meal that Orange either heated up from a box or dumped onto the counter from the nearest fast-food grease pit.

My mind thickened the plot.

Between commercials, Joe would say, "So honey, how many fucked up people did you deliver to the psycho house today?"

"It's so hard to keep track. They all just run together—"

Orange stops her sentence because America's Funniest Home Videos has come back on the screen.

Audibly, I laugh in the backseat of the maroon van.

This family's sad life is the funniest home video I've ever seen.

Despite Orange's carelessness, Joe's dullness, and Shannon's selfishness, I was the one enclosed by metal bars with the key to my freedom dangling from the van's ignition. This van was Orange's domain - her Kingdom -, and I was just a peasant.

In the words of Royal, I was just a delivery.

This was one of the most frightening days of my life. In fact, the maroon van's backseat probably held thousands of people, all of whom had experienced their most frightening day while sitting in the metal cage.

To Orange and Royal, it was just another day on the job. They had no interest in talking to me because they see tens of versions of me every day: hundreds a week, probably.

Orange was concerned with her daughter getting lunch at school, not the comfort of someone else's daughter who sat in the van's backseat. Royal cared about batting averages, pre-season, and whether or not this week's paycheck would give him the extra cash to buy a new Royal's jersey, not if the package he and his partner were delivering was too hot or too cold.

As long as the package gets to where it belongs, their job is done, and it's on to the next emergency room to scoop up the next human bundle of problems. Except for today, Shannon needed lunch. Poor thing couldn't go starving or, even worse, eat cafeteria food!

The van stopped. The back door slid open. Orange pulled out the keys and unlocked my cage. If I had wings, I would have soared out like a dove at an overly-priced, cliché wedding.

I didn't have wings, and I wasn't at a wedding.

I had arrived at the private mental hospital where I would be staying for five days, even though I didn't know that at the time. I stepped out of the van and looked back at the empty seat, the imprint of my rear is still visible on the cheap, tan leather. I hoped that one day Shannon would be in that seat. Maybe then Orange wouldn't see the packages she delivered as things. Maybe then she would see her passengers as people whose fears take form right behind her in the backseat.

I had glanced at Orange one last time before I turned my back to the maroon van, scanning her up and down as she leaned against the trunk and poked at her phone with her index finger.

Maybe not.

16

The automated sliding glass doors opened to a lobby with a marble front desk, an abundance of plants, and a waterfall along the left wall which told my instincts that this was where my ass of a package was going to be dumped. Only spas, fancy hotels, and mental hospitals have waterfalls.

By this time, my dad was standing by my side, holding onto my arm with both hands. I couldn't tell if he was supporting himself or me.

A woman came out from behind the marble counter.

"We've been expecting you, Miss Fritz. Would you please follow me through these doors?"

Her smile and cheery demeanor were out of place in my whirlwind of newfound hatred at Orange.

"I need to assess you before we can go any further."

Her voice was nice, but it was her words I didn't buy. She began guiding me to the back while my dad nearly begged for the woman to wait for my mom to give me a hug before I went in.

"After I assess her, I will bring her back out here, and we can all proceed together," the woman promised.

It was a lie.

My mom was letting Holly relieve herself on one of the bushes that lined the outside of the facility when the lobby door shut, automatically locking behind the lady with the out of place cheer and me.

After 15 minutes of standing in the lobby, my dad realized he wasn't going to get the goodbye hug that he would've killed to have.

17

It was cold. Not the cold that soothed your heated tears or inflamed muscles but the cold that bit your skin with each movement you dared made and sprinted through your soul as a reminder that even something as invisible as temperature could kill you.

The walls were a blue-grey hue as if someone painted them to be gray and then decided that was too depressing for the society-ridden, "depressed" individuals to endure. The result: a paintbrush that splattered blue on the walls in hopes of covering the mistake.

It didn't work. The walls of the room still ached of sadness, just like the bones that outlined my being.

The woman stepped in behind me, clipboard in hand. In the confines of this small, sad room, she seemed larger: domineering. She asked if I wanted something to drink. Without thinking, I gave her an answer. Within five minutes she returned with a water bottle labeled with the institution's name and filled with the cranberry juice that I had apparently asked for. I stared at the bottle that had already started dripping sweat.

I didn't even like cranberry juice.

She asked me a series of questions that ranged from how well I slept to whether or not I wanted to kill myself. Can you imagine? The chair's plastic-like material clung to my skin. My clothes had drops of blood on them and had been with me from my bathroom to the emergency room, and now to this evaluation room. The obviously once-grey walls began to close in, and with each attempt at self-explanation came a chorus of gagging sobs.

"Do you want to kill yourself, Miss Fritz?" She clicked her pen.

"No! I'm just frustrated. I'm not getting the help I need. Why can no one see this!?"

I couldn't remember the last time I screamed at someone in authority. To my surprise, it didn't make me feel better.

Her pen met her chin. She clicked her pen several times. She was toying with the idea of whether or not I would be a patient of this private mental institution. An institution that I would call "The Fix" not because it fixed me but because the facility functioned like a factory created to fix all the problems of any basket case that crossed its threshold. These patients would become "Files."

The Fix didn't care about a patient's mind; it cared about how a patient looked on paper. These papers were put into each patient's very own file. The investors, backers, and most of the Fix's staff focused on the files, not the people explicitly described and analyzed within them.

How many Files could the Fix spew back out into the world each day? How quick was the Fix's fix rate? These are the questions that mattered. These are the questions that predicted profit.

It was a quick fix place, made by a twisted fuck who decided to do a business and turn a profit on society's mangled minds. Files weren't patients, and patients weren't people. Files were dollar signs, and dollar signs were important.

Of course, I wouldn't know this until I completed my five-day vacation at the Fix, a vacation that would start with the last pen click of the click-happy analyst. I was now a File.

All too quickly, the air left my lungs. Gasping, I questioned how I got here.

18

How did I get here?

It only took three months of generic antidepressant prescriptions from my general practitioner to unravel me to the point of intentionally harming myself - three months of trying a new drug every two to three weeks, and I was let down every time. With every letdown, the depression got worse. Unfortunately, life doesn't stop or even slow down just because you're depressed. You're expected to push on, keep working, keep studying, keep socializing, and keep being yourself before the demons of depression shackle you in their web of misery and confusion.

Although I was seven hours away from my home and my parents in Dallas, I had another sort of family in Kansas.

Chessa and Skylar occupied the remaining two rooms in the four-bedroom apartment that Hannah and I lived in. Our apartment was messy and dysfunctional. Besides four college girls, the apartment also housed three cats and one dog. If you imagine a zoo, then you have perfectly captured the essence of our humble abode.

While therapists or doctors or outsiders may say that our friendship, our apartment, and our unusually honest and blunt relationship with one another may be unhealthy, I call horseshit.

Of course, we fight. Of course, we annoy each other. Yes, sometimes Hannah doesn't put my clothes back in my closet. I will admit that I take Chessa's toilet paper when I run out. We can't help but take screenshots of the cute Snapchats that Skylar accidentally sends to us instead of her boyfriend because it is too funny, and everyone needs a good old fashioned piece of blackmail on their best friends. There aren't many boundaries, meaning we steal each other's food all the time. The only thing that is sacred is energy drinks. We aren't total savages.

Despite my support system in Dallas, and despite living with the three strongest women I'll ever meet, I was still depressed. I continued to toss and turn in the middle of the night. I sometimes would sit up and begin to move towards Hannah's door to climb into her bed in hopes that her body heat would scorch the demons out of me.

I always stopped right in front of her closed bedroom door.

The demons were seeping into my brain. Thoughts of bothering Hannah, bothering any of them, pestering them, and eventually losing them, swarmed my conscious.

Train of Guilt-Ridden Thought right on schedule.

Toot! Toot!

I would go back to my bed, lay back down, and let the demons devour me night after night and day after day. It was more tolerable than the thought of losing my three soulmates.

Demons are hungry. They never stop feeding. In three months' time, they stopped feeding on my insides because there was nothing left.

That's when the razor was introduced, like a sheep-slaughtering for sacrifice.

I thank God every day that Hannah, Chessa, and Skylar have hearts of lions. They may never know how many times they saved my life both before that night and countless nights after.

Without even realizing, my breathing had returned to normal, and the click-happy analyst came back into view.

Some people say that their significant other is the wind beneath their wings, but you won't ever hear me saying that.

Instead, and even better, my three best friends are the air in my lungs when life hits me with a low blow to the gut. They're the overly-invested fans cheering me on from the sidelines, even if I am 0-20.

This was it: the ultimate battle with me taking on Depression in the center ring. I was the underdog, odds against me, with outsiders anticipating my fall.

Falling doesn't mean you've been defeated. You've been defeated when you don't get back up again.

I had to get up. I had to. For Skylar. For Chessa. For Hannah. For Mom. For Dad.

For Me.

19

It was frigid. That's what sticks out in my mind the most. In the five days, I was there; I can't recall ever feeling warm.

I stood at the front desk. No one acknowledged me. The Fix was new, and staffing was still being sorted out. As long as the ward had the most up-to-date vending machine, the Fix was good and ready to open, even if that meant having two staff members oversee five clinically psychotic women—six if I felt in the mood to identify myself as such.

My emotions had shut down. They had endured too much. I smirked at the fact that even in a mental hospital I would continue to go unnoticed and untreated.

I was half wrong.

A staff member who didn't look much older than me was the first person I saw when I walked into my ward.

She was short—my height actually—and had a pixie haircut. She was slender and wore a lime green, zip-up hoodie with white strings. Her eyes were the same color as mine, but, instead of sorrow and dullness, hers were as vibrant as her jacket.

By then I had grown accustomed to being looked at in the infamous ways that normal people look at Files before they become Files. Looks filled with hatred from my peers who took my disinterest in their lives as snobbish no longer phased me. Eyes of confusion, eyes of curiosity, and eyes of pity were accounted for daily. Second-take gazes from lustful souls who wanted nothing more than my physical body no longer insulted me. My insides would laugh at them hysterically.

If they wanted my body, they could have it; I was rid of it, anyway.

The staff worker with the lime green jacket with white strings didn't look at me in any of those ways. Suddenly, I was now the one sporting a look of confusion and curiosity.

At first, I pegged it for pity. That wasn't it.

The staff worker with the lime green jacket with the white strings looked at me as if she knew that not much separated her and I except for a key card that opened all of the facility's doors and a razor blade that happened to carve into my skin one too many times.

She looked at me like I was human.

Fuck. I didn't even see myself as human, yet here she was doing what I couldn't.

My blood began to heat with anger. Whether it was targeted at my inability or her capability, I would never know for sure. In spite of the chilling environment, my cheeks flushed pink with spite; the first of many heinous emotions this facility would wage onto my decaying soul.

20

A few magically-opened doors later, courtesy of the employee keycard wand, the staff worker with the lime green jacket with white strings and I were in a medical examination room. By this time, the whole hospital aesthetic was becoming tiresome to my snarky and severely depressed brain.

I sat down on the examination table that was covered with the medical film wrap that is known to make appearances at doctor's offices. My thighs settled on top of the protective sheet and instantaneously produced the sound of a crisp crunch.

Crunch.

The walls were orange with yellow trim that incorporated dancing circus animals. The giraffe always caught my eye because it reigned over the other animals in height, something I would always lack. My mom sat across from me, flipping through a three-month-old edition of *Better Homes & Gardens* magazine. My feet dangled high above the white tiled floor.

Crunch.

My throat was on fire, and each breath brought to life a cough that would make my sides ache and further fan the flames in my esophagus. It was March, and I had already seen the dancing circus animals four times that year. He was going to do the throat thing. I knew he would; he always did. He was going to stick that wooden stick down my throat because that's what doctors did when kids like me had strep-throat. The doctor came in. My mom restrained me, and I squirmed, wailed, and cried out promises to never ask for allowance again. I wasn't strong enough. Moments later, a lollipop was in my mouth, and the doctor had a new bruise on his face for tomorrow.

I looked over and saw the toy chest that was consistently filled with thick wooden books that I was told were supposed to have holes in them to "encourage play and imagination." My mind couldn't compute why something was created to have holes in it, so I finished my lollipop, collected my princess sticker, and left.

The closing of a large wooden door jolted me back from my childhood memory, accompanied by the sound of heels clacking on the popular choice of white tile.

I didn't have a lollipop, there were no princess stickers in my future, and even though I still didn't understand why things were created to have holes in them, I sat on the examination table realizing that time had turned me into just that - a thing ridden with misunderstood gaps.

Along with her high heels, the doctor at this mental institution had piercing blue eyes, a light pink button down that was neatly tucked into her bedazzled jeans, and long blonde hair that fell around her leathery, sun-damaged face. Now technically being a mental patient, I abandoned the social politeness that normal people aren't exempt from and told her that she looked like she took care of horses, not people.

"Well, I do, sweet pea. Examining you is just my side job," she said.

She flashed me her shining, obviously-bleached teeth and laughed at her joke.

So much for using the insanity card to my social advantage.

My snarky persona dissolved as it quickly became clear why I was in the examination room. Not only did reality hit hard, but it also hit low.

This was a strip search.

I was standing stark naked on that white tile floor within minutes. T

he high-heeled, misplaced veterinarian and the staff worker in the lime green jacket with white strings lifted my arms, nudged my legs, and examined every inch of skin that I was unsuccessful at cutting myself out of despite my attempts.

They weren't looking for drugs or weapons. They were recording my current injuries, primarily the ones I had inflicted on myself in my bathtub the day before.

Every scratch, every cut, every open wound, jotted down in a manila folder that I would later realize to be my file. This file would pervasively gain thickness during my residency at the facility.

I never knew the power four eyes could have on my soul until I was forced to strip down and have every bump, scratch, cut, and a scar on my shell of skin accounted for. Once again, only the physicality of my being was looked at. Once again, the outside was being looked at intensely, while my insides were lying away rotting with no one even throwing me a bone of love, attention, or pity.

Once again, the ever impending thought that I was of no value began to solidify. My soul was sick - terminally ill - but the only thing that had been examined over the last five months was my body whose only signs of imperfection were the ones I purposely sliced into my wrists.

Tears began to stream down my cheeks, around my neck, and eventually onto the white tile floor. Neither of the women in the room offered me Kleenex.

I lost my dignity and the feeling in my toes during my naked analysis. I would only gain one back anytime soon.

21

Hannah's workout bag sat on the counter of the nurse's station. At that moment, I appreciated the farce that this bag represented. Hannah didn't work out. On the contrary, she was an advocate for anything that required minimal movement, maximum food, and ideally no pants. Despite having three women unapologetically staring and the slow but painful tingling of feeling returning to my feet, Hannah had somehow managed to make me laugh. My laugh may have outwardly taken the form of a twitch in my cheek, but a riot of laughter and snarky remarks at the expense of Hannah's ludicrous persona erupted inside me.

Her gym bag rested on the counter of the half-circle desk that took up about a quarter of my ward. Behind the counter, there were supposed to be at least two nurses present at all times, "supposed to" being the key phrase. There were three office phones, two cordless home phones, three desktops, countless locked drawers, and file cabinets. This sector of the facility had five rooms. Each room was designed to have two inhabitants allowing the ward to have a maximum of ten patients. Out of those ten beds, only five (six including myself) were occupied during my stay.

To coincide with the lack of consistency to protocol, the inadequately trained and way-in-over-their-head staff members the temperature of the ward was unwaveringly frigid. The common space floors were, of course, white tile, while the bedroom floors were a dark wood. Each of the five bedrooms had thick doors with a light wood finish, and behind each door, one would find two beds, two desks, two closets, and a wooden trunk at the foot of each bed that could only be opened by a key. Each bed had one pillow, cream sheets that were still new and stiff, and a green blanket that was as itchy as it was useless when combating the cold at night.

Space was simple, minimalistic, and clean. The only sign of clutter and excess was the back wall behind the main counter. This monstrosity of a wall was riddled with shelves, each shelf containing stacks upon stacks of neatly placed manila folders, one of them labeled with my name. The back wall also had a door inserted in its structure. The door led to a small room that was filled with any pharmaceutical drug you could fathom: uppers, downers, in-betweeners; this compact space was a drug addict's wet dream. A small glass window was the only way patients could see inside. It was through this small glass window that residents of my ward were given the gift of sleep, the pleasure of focus, the joy of energy, the relief of pain, the lull of inner voices bickering, and the assurance of reality. It was through this window that, three times a day, pills would find their way descending down my throat in hopes of assuaging my inner turmoil.

Lining up at that glass window was lining up for battle. Three times a day I would begrudgingly conjure up the will to live and continue experimenting with medications. Three times a day I was forced to wrestle with the unbearable possibility that once again, whatever new pill they handed me wouldn't diminish my emotional distress. Three times a day I was bound to combat for my existence when I had nothing but dashed hopes and self-aimed disgust.

Three times a day I went to battle, and three times a day I lost.

Instead, each walk to the window, each swallowed pill, each swig of water, each crushed cup, prompted fragments of hope to break off my soul and fall to the knees of the darkness that consumed me.

In reality, three times a day the nurse would watch me walk to the window, reach my hand out, grab the pills, swallow the water, crush the paper cup, put it in the trashcan, and proceed to my room. Reality never met my psyche at that glass window during the five days that made up my mental hospital excursion.

On the first night when I was admitted, my fixation of the gym bag that had never seen a gym caused me to overlook the glass window of warfare. With the exception of meals, the glass window was the only terror I would be spared from that night. Tomorrow the glass window would rupture my soul, but, for my first night, I was safe within the boundaries of my room which was assigned to me after the girl with the lime green jacket with white strings cataloged each item that she plucked out of my bag.

One by one, my existence beyond the hospital's walls was condensed to the items in Hannah's gym bag. At that moment, the familiarity of my clothes in that bag possessed an alarming level of importance. The only avenue of comfort available to me while standing at the ward's desk was through my clothing. Unfortunately, comfort wouldn't find me through the t-shirts, sweats, hoodies and athletic shorts that the girl with the lime green jacket with white strings arranged on the counter. She made no record any of my favorite clothes because none of my favorite clothes were present. A flashback of my bloodied wrists and Hannah shoving fragments of my closet into her bag convinced me to swallow my frustration at Hannah's lack of care during the selection process of my clothes.

My frustration had fully dissipated and, instead, had taken the shape of shock when the girl with the lime green jacket with white strings began extracting the strings from my hoodies and sweatpants.

Why the hell did she get strings in her hoodie and I didn't?

The answer was waiting for me in my room.

22

I took the gym bag loaded with my stringless wardrobe to my new bedroom. Relief surged through my body when I realized I didn't have a roommate. That was when I felt the urge to relieve my bladder. For a second I found myself envious that Holly got to go outside and I didn't.

The sink's handles generated water for only a calculated number of seconds before its flow was stopped. The upward curvature of the wall's towel hooks recoiled towards the floor if any pressure other than the weight of a wet towel was placed upon them. The sink's basin was a height calculated to allow only hands under the faucet. The towels were a calculated length that left little room to cover anything other than the body parts used for procreation. The showerhead came directly out of the tiled wall leaving it without a neck. The room's furniture was rid of sharp corners and replaced with rounded ones.

The link between these oddities and my wardrobe's lack of strings collided as the realization of the morbid logic of the facility's masterminds and undertakers sucker punched my chest.

The sink's handles were calculated to prevent the flow of water large enough for a deliberate drowning. The hooks were calculated to fold at the stress of knotted strings that latched around a human's neck and carried the body's weight. Purposeful suffocation was expunged with the showerhead's lack of neck and my hoodie's lack of strings. The basin was calculated to omit the placement of a human's head under the faucet for intentional lack of air. The towels were calculated to ensure a double knotted suicide bow around a one's neck would never come to life and instead, remain a morbid idea. The furniture's curved edges were calculated to diminish the presence of deliberate cuts.

In a room safety proofed for death, I had never envisioned it more.

23

The room started to spin. Tears started to brim. I tried breathing, but the world didn't have any oxygen left. Who had taken it all?

There was a white pill, a cup of water, and the girl with the lime green jacket with privileged white strings.

I swallowed the pill without the water. The water cup seemed too heavy, and my throat had been rid of feeling since I was sworn into the Fix. The girl with the lime green jacket with privileged white strings guided me to my bed. She wrapped my body in the puke green burrito of itchy wool and placed my head on the pillow that might as well have been the floor. Regardless, my body succumbed to the little white pill, and my eyelids began their descent. Thank God. I couldn't stand to see anymore. I fell asleep to the sound of someone laughing hysterically. The laughter faded into a giggle, and it wasn't until right before I fell asleep that I realized where it was coming from.

Me.

24

The Fix didn't give its occupants alarm clocks. Instead, Files got a breakfast roundup from Cub.

"You'll miss breakfast if you don't get up. Next chance won't be 'til lunch, and I doubt you'll want to miss breakfast. This morning its biscuits and gravy!" he said.

This was my first encounter with Cub. I stumbled out of bed only to instantly regret it when my feet hit the (not surprisingly) cold floor. Everything in this goddamn place was cold.

Cub, or whoever was on morning duty for the day, would round me and the other psychotically disturbed cattle to the entrance of the Fix's "Good Side," count us off and then scan the magic card to begin the 27-step journey to the cafeteria. Trust me, I counted.

Cub wasn't his real name, but he resembled a stump: short, chubby, tub-like. He waddled when he walked, and it was clear that the height was something he was born with; the weight was a recent addition due to middle age. I suspected that he wrestled in high school. Days later I found out that I'm a damn good guesser.

Cub was real, unlike the clipboard-holding, pen-clicking dominatrix that wrote my body into the Fix's custody as she flashed those pearly whites into an unwavering smile. Cub would smile but not too hard and not too often. He laughed in a simple chuckle or rolled his eyes while exhaling heavy air when a patient said something funny or was acting like a total basket case. He didn't tiptoe around us like we were China dolls that could break if he exhaled too hard with one of his eye rolls. He gave each File the credit of having a sense of humor, a sense of reality, and a sense of decency, even if some days we didn't.

In my small way of thanking him, I called him Cub instead of the obvious Chub.

While Cub waited for the stragglers (myself included) to join him at the door with the rest of the Files, I stared at the piece of heavily inked paper on my desk. It wasn't there when I fell to pieces the night before, and it was too obnoxiously decorated to overlook. It must have been placed there while I was fending off hellish nightmares from which I couldn't wake.

It was the day's schedule labeled with meal times, group therapy, music therapy, art therapy, outside time, free time, and visiting hours.

VISITING HOURS!

I threw the printed outline of the day ahead onto my bed as I scurried in response to Cub's last call on breakfast goers. Walking through the Good Side entrance doors to breakfast, Cub witnessed my first genuine smile in the Fix before my upturned lips were wrecked to flatness by a sour realization.

Visiting hours weren't until 7:30 that night, and I had to meet the other Files over biscuits and gravy now.

25

I was the youngest File by a good thirty years. That was easy to tell just by walking behind the herd to the cafeteria.

I was last in line, holding my tray while my eyes scanned. I wasn't looking at the breakfast buffet; I was looking at them.

They looked like moms. Some of them could even pass as grandmothers. Why were they here? They looked so harmless.

One look down at my left forearm, swaddled up to the elbow in gauze was all it took to remind me that I, too, was harmless, just not when it came to my body.

I wasn't granted access to each File's life story at my first breakfast, and some Files never did grant me full access to their history.

Instead, it was over several mornings of biscuits and gravy, multiple group therapy sessions, and during the commercial breaks of whatever reality television show was blaring on the ward's common space TV. These women shared bits and pieces of who they are, who they once were, and who they wanted to be once they were released from the Fix's hold. I quickly learned that the presence of inner warfare raging through their souls (and being born before 1970) was just about the only similarities between each of the Files.

No File had the same background or life outside of the Fix. No File had the same reason for being in the Fix. No File was properly treated while in the Fix.

In the fix, all Files were treated the same.

File 1: Sandra

She checked in the morning after I arrived. Her hair was gray and spiked. Only faded baseball t-shirts seemed to hang from her broad shoulders unless she decided to flaunt her burnt orange hoodie which just so happened to be most of the day every day.

Another fucking orange hoodie. Can you believe that shit?

The hoodie did a lousy and highly misleading job at describing her personality, but it did an ace job at covering the thick, gauze bandaging that enclosed the entirety of her left forearm. I assumed that under the bandages were a single vertical scar, forming what would soon be the fossil of a cut so gruesome that it carried the ability to execute an ample amount of physical damage without the assistance of another wound. Once again, I was a damn good guesser.

Sandra appeared abnormally familiar with the procedures, rules, and setup of the facility. She knew what she was allowed to bring with her during her stay, exactly where the mobile phones were located to call friends and family, and exactly when they distributed morning, afternoon, and nighttime medications. Adversely, I spent my first night crying to such an extremity that I emerged the next morning with swollen eyes that carried hints of pink around the edges. I couldn't fathom how another woman could not be jolted in the slightest when faced with being admitted into a mental facility.

Sandra wasn't a talker. She didn't speak to any other patients until her third day. She would only speak to staff if it regarded her medicine, the TV channel, meals, or family and friend visitations. The only occasion where Sandra showed any emotion during the four days when I was, by default, a part of her existence was when it came to visitation. Every day she asked the nurses if she would have a guest, and every day on the phone she inquired about whether or not someone, in particular, was coming.

I eventually learned that the person Sandra was consistently asking about was the girl she was in love with. Sandra had met her at this same mental institution only a few months prior. To Sandra, it was love. To the recipient of Sandra's affections, Sandra was a coping mechanism to make the group therapy, medication changes, and safety restrictions slightly more bearable. Sandra fell in love in this ward, and now she was back, this time as a physically and emotionally torn apart woman.

Sandra wanted to die because she was in love with a woman who didn't love her back.

File 2: Betty

Betty had a slight country accent and thick, round-rimmed glasses. She was one of those 55-year-old ladies who you automatically knew was gorgeous back in her twenties, despite whatever atrocious hairstyle was trending at that time. Betty always wore white or light pinks and grays. Her clothes always looked soft, just like her face. Unlike Sandra, Betty loved to talk. Without hesitation, she would fill any silence that tried to emerge during group therapy which was a relief if you didn't want to talk that day but a panic attack in the making if you needed to unload your thoughts. She hugged me within five minutes of seeing my puffy eyelids that morning because that was just the type of person she was. At that moment she reminded me of my mom.

Sometimes her words were comforting and encouraging, but, more often than not, the things she spewed out were so outlandishly off-topic and erratic that, even in a mental hospital, the other ladies and I couldn't help but laugh. Regardless of what she was talking about, not once did Betty raise her voice. Regardless of another patient's obvious rudeness to her, Betty was never phased or discouraged.

Betty owned a farm with her husband and had a good handful of children. Her children had also spawned grandchildren who she talked to once on our ward's mobile phone. She talked to them in a baby voice that made the patients, and even the nurses on duty that night, laugh hysterically. Even if she didn't realize it at the time, that phone call did more for any of us than it did for Betty or her grandchildren. If she had realized it, I'm sure she would have wanted it that way.

Betty got married when she was 19 years old and had her first of several babies by the time she was twenty. I wondered whether I would have preferred to have a baby in my arms at twenty or scars on my arms at twenty. I made my decision based on the conclusion that I don't have to feed my scars or find a babysitter for my arm anytime I go out for the night.

Betty never traveled outside the U.S., and she never saw the ocean. Betty never had a career or went to pursue a college degree. Instead, Betty put her efforts into what she did have - her family.

She put her husband first. She put the farm and the animals first. She put her kids and her grandkids first. With so many things that came first, Betty came last. Betty was so far down the order of importance that, when a bottle of pain meds presented themselves, she gobbled them as though everyone else's life depended on it because she no longer cared about her own.

Betty wanted to die because she had never fully lived.

File 3: Torrance

Torrance fits in with the group of women in the ward as well as your hand fits in the bottom of a Pringle's can; she just doesn't.

Lines indented into her skin encircled her consistently pursed lips. Later I would learn that, decades prior, her lips were pursed in concentration over medical books under dusty university lamps. The concentration that resulted in pressured lines around her thin lips also resulted in a doctoral degree with her name on it. What was once a possession of hard work was now a symbol of negligence as dust clung to the crookedly-hung piece of paper.

That is how Torrance saw herself.

All accounts of Torrance are lucid in my brain because she was so unbelievable that I unknowingly made it a point to store every detail deep within my cluttered wall of mental manila folders. She walked into the common space on my second day after lunch. I had no idea she existed, but she did exist, and God almighty she wished she didn't.

Picture the ideal grandmother, then add a white pullover with the image of a young girl forever frozen mid-spin on an ice rink printed smack dab in the center. That was Torrance.

The first time I saw my long-lost grandmother emerge from her room, her face looked groggy. Imprints of the bed sheets on her face only enhanced her exhausted aura. Torrance shuffled to the front desk. Betty leaned over the table where I sat reading the same sentence of one of the books from the library.

I'll never get anything done here was my thought that Betty interrupted.

"She swallowed a bunch of Xanax. Poor thing shoved them right down her gullet. Apparently, the Chinese food delivery guy found her and called 911. This is the first time she's been up."

Torrance wouldn't talk for the next two days. Not only did the amount of Xanax she took to do a real number on her, but by nature, she wasn't a very talkative person. She observed, and she studied which is how she got her doctorate in psychology.

Torrance knew more about the human mind than the nurses that babysat us. Torrance knew just as much as, or even more than, the psychiatrists that wrote our ever-changing scripts and the therapists that pretended to relate to our problems.

The girl on her sweatshirt was her only daughter who had been a figure skater until she went to college, got married, and moved far away, despite her mother's old age. Torrance's husband had died decades before she decided it was her turn.

Her body was old, but her mind was sharp. She was quick and picked up every detail made available to her. It was when her vacuum of a mind sucked up the signs of abandonment from her daughter that she decided to hoard three months' worth of her Xanax prescription and feast on them all at once. Her last supper.

Her last meal was not Chinese food from the Chinese delivery guy. That was not part of the plan. She was sure that no one would come over. No one had for three months!

Delivery Guy had the wrong address, Torrance never locked her front door, and Delivery Guy was so eager for a tip that he took the liberty of opening an unlocked front door.

The only tip Delivery Guy got was to always double check the address. You might find a barely-conscious senior woman lying on the floor.

Torrance wanted to die because she already felt dead to her daughter.

File 4: Amber

Unlike Sandra's hoodie, Amber's name perfectly matched her long hair. Unlike Torrance, Amber's mind was not always the clear crystal ball that she thought it was. Unlike Betty, Amber didn't have any family.

Amber's affections were to cigarettes, and it reflected in the rasp of her voice. She wasn't talkative or quiet; she talked just the right amount. She was younger than Torrance but older than everyone else, or maybe it was just the cigarettes that made her look that way.

Amber contradicted the belief that the older you get, the wiser you become. Now, whether it was a number of drugs she had gulped down her throat, injected up her veins, and snorted up her nostrils, or rather the lack of a formal education and decent childhood upbringing that most people like to believe every adolescent gets, it was obvious that Amber's bad hand of cards came with the betting price of her intelligence.

That woman must have lost to a Royal Flush because the dealer known as life took her for all she had, even if the pot wasn't that much to start out with.

Her memory slips were manageable in small doses: easy to shake off and forget.

"Where is my headband?" she asked several times during my stay.

Several times it was on her head.

Her lapses weren't always so minor. More than once, confusion would sweep over her like a tsunami over an already-struggling Third World country. Suffocation, terror, and darkness were the recipe of merciless waves that washed away periods of her memory. Sometimes it would be a few hours. Sometimes she would forget entire days. One time, she forgot why she was in the Fix and not at home in her recliner. No matter how far back the tsunami of confusion swept her memory, the result was the same: a bewildered pair of eyes with the rims full of tears that may or may not fall down her cheek's tattered skin, her lips mouthing for a cigarette and or pills.

Amber wanted to die because life no longer made sense.

File 5: Tess

She was by far the most lucid of the Files which, ironically, caused her to have the thickest file out of our ward. She was Jewish, hysterically belligerent, and fabulous which is hard to do when stuck in the Fix or any other place like it. You could always hear Tess before you saw her. The sight of her wasn't so bad either. She wasn't stunning, but the Fix didn't allow makeup, so technically none of us were given a chance to look like anything but mentally ill women, trudging our feet to the feeding trough in our bathrobes and uncombed hair.

All dolled up in a cocktail dress, Tess could easily go an entire night out on the town without paying for a single drink. But in a fix the cafeteria's harsh lights hit the top of her scalp, revealing the mix of brown and gray roots that intruded on the rest of her bleach blonde hair.

"Staring is rude. Also, roots are in now, don't you know?" were the first words Tess spoke to me. In fact, they were the first words spoken to me by anyone during my inaugural breakfast.

I must've been staring hard for her to have not only noticed my staring from the cold cereal station of the buffet assembly line, but also for her to have said something.

Fuck me. I haven't even put my tray down.

Tess was intimidating, but the façade would only stick if you were on her hit list. Her coarse humor, sharp wit, and loud mouth that ran quicker than Usain Bolt himself surprisingly matched my sarcasm and appreciation for dark humor.

When I think of the times I did laugh while admitted into the Fix, Tess was usually the source, but it was a just after eight in the morning on my first full day in the Fix's encampment. Tess and I didn't become friends until noon.

Her tray of biscuits and gravy was adjacent from mine. Not only at this breakfast but during the entirety of my stay, Tess consistently wore designer sweats and cardigans and pullovers that I expected to cost a semester's worth of my textbooks. Two gold necklaces never left her neck. They clanked together as she walked around. The gold charms clapping together created a sound of appraisal, Tess's constant applause. To top it of

f, her nail beds were replaced by square cut acrylics that wouldn't take out your eye if she swiped, but they may take out your sight just as a friendly reminder that she could if she wanted to.

Tess's story tumbled out that morning all over my biscuits and gravy, and boy was she eager to tell it.

Tess exuded money, but none of it belonged to her.

Tess's husband was a lawyer and a damned good one at that. Tess and Lawyer had two kids. It was after she dropped their two kids off at soccer practice that she planned to drive to her usual bar with a bountiful medley of drugs tucked in her purse; most of which could be found in the nightstand of any housewife who has too much free time on her manicured hands and too much of her husband's money to know what to blow it on.

Most blow it on blow, according to Tess. They slide on their Jimmy Choo's, mount their 8-miles-to-the-gallon SUV, drive to the "bad part" of town, and dig into their Chanel bags to pull out their allowance of Ben Franklins in exchange for a blizzard in July.

"I'm not like that, though," she scoffed as if there was a competition to see which pampered housewife could do drugs the coolest.

"I may have money, but at least I have originality, for Christ's sake!" Tess did a quick scan to see whose attention she captured. Amber, Betty, and I couldn't help but get sucked into Tess's vacuum of theatrics.

Unamused, Sandra sat across the cafeteria at her table with her orange eye-sore of a back facing ours. Torrance seemed to share Sandra's lack of interest and didn't bother looking up from her tray, despite Tess sitting two chairs away. Instead, Torrance salted her biscuits and gravy for what seemed like the twentieth time in the two-minute span of her sitting down.

Can taking over 70 Xanax make you lose your sense of taste?

My thoughts couldn't wander any further than that question because three out of five was a good enough audience for Tess.

"I dropped them off planning to do a Speedball topped off with some gin." She threw her head back and laughed at the words that she would spew out next. "I figured my husband would then have to do TWO new things that night: pick up the fucking kids and talk to them!" She laughed so hard that no noise came out of her mouth, and she rocked back and forth as if to regain her composure. Her necklaces swayed and applauded her comedic genius.

"The bastard's first conversation with them would be to tell em' that their mother's dead! Can you fucking imagine?!"

This time her polished nails curled around her plastic fork and her fist pounded onto the table as she let out another howl of laughter. She looked like a baby in a highchair hammering away at the counter top with her infant-sized silverware.

The lawyer did have to pick up the kids that day, and he did have to talk to them, but those were the only firsts he had to do.

Less than a mile from her glass of gin, Tess made an illegal U-turn, threw her Prada bag of cocaine, Xanax, and Hydrocodone in the back seat, and screeched into the Fix's parking lot. You could see her Cadillac SUV placed diagonally over two parking spots from the cafeteria's window wall.

"I checked myself in."

These words didn't come with a volcano of laughter, a knee slap, or a grin. Even

her two biggest fans around her neck were mute. The wealthy, somewhat blonde lady who had intimidated me minutes ago wasn't there anymore. Instead, a woman who could shatter to pieces if the wind blew too hard sat in front of me.

Tess wanted to die because, despite having everything, she had nothing to live for.

"Alright. Put your trays up. Let's go ladies. Other sectors gotta eat too."

Cub's voice echoed. For such a small man, his voice was rather big.

I followed the Files who followed Cub to the cafeteria exit and through the 27-step long hallway until we reached our ward.

WAIT. WHAT?

I grabbed Betty's arm, knowing that she was always more than eager to help a hurt bird or lost puppy. Lucky for her, at that moment, I looked like both.

"Betty, is there another section?"

"Why, of course, darlin'." Her voice sounded like mama's homemade molasses with a southern twist, but I didn't have the patience for molasses-speed answers. I responded with a Please-Do-Go-On-You-Know-That-Answer-Doesn't-Do-Me-Any-Good look.

"It's right through that hallway. That's how the nurses can go back and forth between the sectors in case they need backup." Betty's right index finger pointed to another door that I didn't know existed until her finger made it appear.

"Backup?" I said, wincing.

"Oh, honey." She paused to look at me. Right before I jumped out of my skin, her molasses voice whispered, "That's the Dark Side."

That sentence, despite being covered in Betty's honey-sweet voice, made my stomach hit a sour note.

I walked to my bathroom, knelt over the toilet, and had my biscuits and gravy all over again.

26

In case they need backup. In case they need backup. In case they need backup.

There was nothing left for my stomach to give, but my mind wasn't made. I dry heaved for what felt like hours over the suicide-proof toilet. Reality would later tell me that it had only been seven minutes.

My ward was Green Valley. The other ward was Blue Skies. No one called the wards by their fantasy preschool names unless one of the Suits who owned a fair share of the joint decided it was a good day to see how well he was doing at profiting off the mentally ill through the perverted (but undeniably profitable) fix-em'-quick-and-ship-em-out strategy.

When it was just the Files and the nurse babysitters, the awards were known as the Good Side and the Dark Side. The only thing separating the two worlds was a set of doors, a narrow hallway, and another set of doors, all of which had been laid out for my viewing pleasure by Betty's pointer finger.

The afternoon of my first full day in the Fix, a woman nurse broke through this set of doors into the Good Side, her only possible point of origin being the Dark Side.

She walked like a little kid at the public pool who wanted to run to the diving board but was just whistled at and told to walk, resulting in an awkward shuffle that was neither walking nor running but somewhere uncomfortably in between.

Amber, Tess and I were a few feet away watching the common room TV. The nude man on the screen attempted to start a fire in the woods, but his large biceps and tribal tattoos weren't going to help him out of this pickle. Amber's eyes were on the TV, but it didn't seem like anything was going past her headband. Tess snacked on a 100 calorie snack pack even though breakfast was 30 minutes ago.

"I could never be on this show," she would say between shoveling mini cookies into her mouth. "The only thing I'm afraid of is being naked on TV." She chuckled, making her chest shake. Her necklaces applauded her commentary.

"He threw a chair, Tom. A fucking chair."

The poor nurse was trying to be quiet, but she failed miserably. They probably should've rethought all tile, all marble, all hardwood décor when building this echoing cathedral of depression. The on-duty babysitter who was apparently named Tom left his post at the nurses' counter and grabbed an ice pack from the prescription room for his injured coworker. Tom was graying but not all the way gray yet (he had maybe one more year left) and had only one ear pierced with an earring that had a small diamond dangling from the main stud. I bet he played the electric guitar in a band back in the 80's called 21 Crimes or something close to it.

Tess turned to me. Her eyes glistened with excitement, but I didn't like the feeling it gave my already-emptied stomach.

"If you had to pick one, would you rather be getting furniture tossed at you, like Shuffles over there from the Dark Side, or be a contestant on *Naked and Afraid*?" she asked.

"What's so bad over there? I don't get it," I said, purposely not answering her morbid question. Later I would find the dark humor funny, but the joke was still too ripe at the time.

Tess didn't even have to laugh this time; a smirk did just the job.

"Oh, you'll see."

She winked a hazel eye at me and then returned to the cold, naked suckers on the TV screen.

See what?

27

The second day I saw it.

Tess had become the older sister that I never had and never wanted, and I had become a surrogate for the daughter that she had back home. She braided my hair. She hugged me whenever I would lose a battle at the prescription window and tears would swell in my eyes. "You'll win the next one," she would say.

We called each other Bitch because we couldn't admit that we were found on each other; "only weaklings show emotions" was our shared thought process. The joke was on us because we were in a goddamn mental hospital. Despite the joke being on us, we liked to make the joke about others.

One of the two therapists at the Fix we openly called Jersey Mike for his greased back, thick hair, tan-in-March skin, and unmistakable East Coast accent. He also wasn't the brightest bulb in the tanning bed. Often, in group therapy, he would write on the dry erase board only to hear a sneer from Tess and an obnoxious cough from me. That's when he would look back at the board for a good twenty seconds until he would finally give up and ask what word he had misspelled.

"It's wrought. W-R-O-U-G-H-T." Poor guy spelled it like a rotten egg.

I couldn't help sounding like a smartass, and in a facility that strips you of all your dignity and makes you question your sanity, knowing how to spell better than the certified therapist makes you feel pretty fucking good.

Tess had a big mouth, and she talked an even bigger game, but she was right about at least one thing, that was for sure.

After dinner on my second day, blue would mix with green and the sky would defy gravity and touch the valley.

Betty had just begun what we all knew was one of her famous group therapy filibusters when a member of the Dark Side appeared in the therapy room's threshold. Jersey Mike wasn't leading group that day, praise the Fix's scheduling gods.

What stood in the doorway was a lot to take in. Easily standing at 6'2" with wild, red, frizzy hair that was tame in comparison to the deranged look in her foggy, green, and overly dilated pupils stood a member of the Dark Side.

"May, take a seat right here."

The voice came from behind this May character. May sat down to reveal the voice's owner: a small, female nurse in puppy dog scrubs.

Not only was May a walking oxymoron with her name of sunshine and demeanor of anger, but she had a fucking nanny, too.

Tess, who sat to my left, clenched my arm and whispered, "Do you see it now?"

Actually, no. I couldn't see it. I couldn't see anything because May had just brought all of her darkness into the room.

I didn't talk in therapy that day.

28

Many of my most horrific memories occurred in cafeterias.

My first embarrassing moment that I can recount from memory was in preschool and occurred in the daycare's cafeteria that doubled as a gymnasium. I was sitting at the only lunch table with my classmates and teacher. It was pizza day, and I wore a white shirt. The lunch man came back asking if anyone asked for seconds, and in a fit of excitement and gluttony, I shoved the remains of the first slice in my mouth so my teacher would let me get a second piece. Before the lunch man could hand me my next piece of pizza, I spit up the entirety of my first slice onto my white shirt. Laughter from my classmates filled my ears, and my tear streaked face wouldn't dare look up. Instead, I looked down chin to chest, at my shirt. It wasn't white anymore. I now sported a shirt whose pizza sauce stains matched the color of my embarrassed face.

Even at the age of 21, with a medical bracelet from an emergency room on my right arm, an identification band as a File of the Fix on the left, and a canopy of self-inflicted scars on both, the Fix's cafeteria was no exception.

The first time I saw Him was in the cafeteria on my third full day as a File. A nurse's watch must've been running fast (or another's must've been running slow) because that day the Dark Side came in while we put away our trays. The idea of different classes being scheduled different meal rotations brought me back to lunch time during my first year of public school, seventh grade.

The school was broken up by wings of the building. The first floor was the zoo where sixth graders terrorized teachers with their immaturity, a byproduct of being overwhelmed by a new school that just so happened to place its newcomers in the basement. The second-floor left wing was the seventh-grade territory. The eighth graders ruled the right wing. Just as grade divided the building, each lunch period was broken up the same. Sixth grade was first, then seventh, ending with the eighth graders. Every day after our 25 minutes of lunch, teachers made us line up with our backs against the poorly painted white brick wall as we waited to be accounted for and use the restroom before we would be escorted in a single file line back to the classroom. My teacher for lunch period that year was Ms. Light which is ironic because lunch was the darkest and most traumatizing daily routine in my 13-year-old mind.

The cafeteria was loud, things echoed, and it smelled like cleaning water mixed with heat from cooking which made the room smell thick and heavy. Without fail, the white tile floors were always decorated with spilled orange juice or some unknown brown colored liquid. It was crowded which left me never to know where to sit or, more importantly, with whom to sit. Often, I was asked to scoot a seat over to make room for someone else, save a seat for someone else, or even find a different table on which to sit so everyone else could sit together. My shy demeanor was not going to be missed at a table of pre-teens who had been having birthday parties together since first grade. I simply didn't bring enough to the table.

When it was time to exit the cafeteria and place our backs against the wall while we were counted off, we could see the eighth graders begin to leave their classes for their turn to eat. They were bigger. They were more defined, not necessarily in muscle or tone but in character. They either looked mean or nice, extraordinarily polished or extraordinarily rough. Regardless of where they fell on the spectrum, they were consistently "more than" what each sixth and seventh grader was. They were idolized and viewed as demigods in the eyes of even the most popular members of the lower grades, demigods that my classmates and I would become once summer began. It was the season where a shift in power occurs that transforms seventh graders into the next school year's middle school demigods, and eighth graders become mortal as a freshman in high school. Because we knew our destiny, we watched them. We watched those eighth graders every chance we could in hopes that we might see the secret trick or power that made our slightly older schoolmates exude such desirable qualities: physical, mental, and emotional.

I stared back and forth between my BBQ sandwich and today's on-duty nurse who landed the lucky role of escorting us in a single file line to lunch. Once there, her responsibility was to write down what each File got from the lunch line, how much the File ate, how fast or slow the File ate, and how the File acted while that File ate. The biography of the File's lunch is recorded in a manila folder by the time the File put the flimsy tray back on the rack.

Sandwich. Her. Sandwich. Her. My eyes kept going between the two until they walked in. Along with them, came Him.

He wore a blue button-down shirt that, even from a distance, highlighted his already big, bold, blue eyes. He had dark hair and a strong chin. To finish the look, he wore black dress pants, a black leather belt, a tie, and a gold wedding band, but His shirt and pants were caked with wrinkles. His tie was tied poorly and would sway across His chest when He moved as a result of it being too loose. His dark hair was graying at the roots and was disheveled in every which way. His strong chin was overpowered by the mayhem of facial hair formed as a result of not shaving His five o'clock shadow. His leather belt was horrible worn, and his blue eyes were unnaturally large and unsettlingly glossy, like a scared puppy. The only thing that remained unscathed was the wedding band, consistently gold and sacred.

Despite all these imperfections, He didn't portray the characteristics or quirks of someone who belonged on the Dark Side whose members had created a uniform line to be served their choice of soup or side salad. He held up the rear.

The line consisted of sociopaths, schizophrenics, hypo-maniacs, and maniacs drooling, twitching, scratching, bursts of aggression, fits of tears, talking loud, talking fast, whispering, and fidgeting. Each person in the lunch line was performing one or more of these actions, except Him. Each person in the lunch line stared at members of my ward with either hate, jealousy, or longing embedded in their eyes. Whether they had tears coming down their cheeks or spit oozing out of their open mouths, they all stared, except Him. Without warning or consent, I was the eighth grader sitting at lunch while a line of seventh graders with medical bracelets studied my every gesture. They had unknowingly bought into the fallacy that, if they watched hard enough and paid close enough attention, then when the season changed with an upgrade to a magical prescription. They would transform into the eighth graders that could eat their lunch together without having a violent outburst or talking to people that weren't present anywhere other than their mind. However, mental health doesn't adhere to the same procedure as grade school. You don't get better because it's summer, and mental health isn't confined to being present only five days a week, seven hours a day. The individuals in the lunch line didn't know that, and I questioned whether or not they ever would.

In a line full of seventh graders, He stood as an adult. Aside from His unfortunate outfit, I couldn't make out why He was getting his lunch with the Dark Side instead of finishing His food with my ward. At the back of that lunch line, He inherently looked like a man standing in line at a coffee shop on His way to work after a night of heavy drinking.

He was getting his BBQ sandwich when my ward's lunch time babysitter closed the manila folder and motioned for my table to get up and head back to our sector for group therapy.

"Just stop talking! It's too many voices! What do you mean you don't like this show?! Well, fuck you!"

A flying fork met the plasma TV that was mounted on the cafeteria wall. Andy Griffith now had ranch dressing and a small piece of lettuce on his forehead.

An overweight woman in her late forties with blonde curls that at one point must have been bouncy and full of life sat at a table eating her salad with a spoon. She sat there, alone, with no one there to prompt or answer her disturbingly clamorous question. She sat there alone, and she smiled. Her smile curled into a giggle, and her giggle evolved into words that she then constructed into conversational sentences that she aimed at either the chair to her right or the chair directly across from her. None of the chairs at her table were occupied, except for hers.

The sound of the fork meeting with the television screen, her fit of anger towards a nonexistent individual (or individuals), her cracked, yellowed teeth that revealed themselves as a product of her giggle of hysteria, refuse to extract themselves from my mind's eye almost a year later.

Her fit of mania did not bring Him to flinch, stumble, or look up from His tray as he walked to a seat at an empty table near the wall of windows. He unfolded His napkin onto his lap and began cutting his sandwich with elegance and grace that I could have only imagined to be a product of years of dining women and corporate sharks. I left the cafeteria with the image of Him slicing His sandwich bun with a plastic knife.

Many of my most horrific memories occurred in cafeterias, but He is my most haunting.

I would see him one more time.

29

Visiting hours showed me more than group therapy did.

Visiting hours were similar to that of a prison. You get called in by the guard - in my case a nurse - and escorted to the cafeteria where the person, or persons, who took time out of the real world had come to visit you for an hour. Hearing of things still occurring, or of people still living life while your own is currently on a medical pause, is uncomfortable, but humbling, realization. The world still goes on with or without you.

The first and third full days of my stay at the Fix, my mom and dad were sitting at the designated cafeteria table, anxiously waiting for me to come in as if there was a question of whether or not I still existed.

The first time, they both cried. The second time, just my mom cried. I didn't cry either time. I could cry in my itchy green blanket and rock hard pillow once my hour time slot with them was up, but I was determined to be happy, or at the very least I would be strong. Within ten minutes of the first visit with my parents, I realized that those two one-hour time slots when I saw them while I was a File of the Fix weren't for me but them.

I was it: their only daughter. Standing in front of them with puffy eyes, no makeup, sweats and an oversized hoodie that covered up the bandages on my forearms that I would routinely catch my dad staring at. I was on full display. I couldn't hide anything anymore.

I was their flesh and blood, and I had damaged both, deeply.

They asked a lot of questions. 75 percent of them I didn't know the answers to, and the other 20 percent I didn't want to answer. As a family, we worked with the spare change: the 5 percent.

Do you want to know if someone loves you? If all you have is 5 percent and they love the hell out of you while they scrape up the remaining 95 - that's love.

On the third day during my second visit with my parents was when I saw Him again.

Just over my Dad's broad right shoulder, He was with her: his wife. They sat two tables behind my parent's back, two tables straight ahead of me.

She looked frail as if she could crumble like Jericho with a clean sweep of her legs.

Thank God she's sitting, I remembered thinking to myself.

The cafeteria echoed, and voices collided in the open tiled space, but I didn't need to hear their conversation for my heart to cave into my chest.

He sat next to her, hand on her knee. He no longer looked like the hungover businessman in line at the coffee shop, but rather a father sitting at the head of his dinner table with his true love at his right side. He was a File, but he looked alive. She wasn't a File, and she looked dead.

He kept motioning and talking to the other side of their designated visiting table, but no one was there. He leaned his elbows onto the table and hunched forward as if to whisper something into Casper the Friendly Ghost's ear from across the table. He even moved his forever-crooked, permanently-wrinkled tie to the side. By the look of his uncomfortably distorted posture, and by the concentration and caution he displayed in delivering his message to Casper, it was as if there was a stream of hot lava running down the center of the table's surface.

There was no hot stream of lava, only a stream of tears from his wife's eyes. He didn't notice. He continued to talk over the lava to Casper.

Her husband's body remained intact, but his mind had unraveled to the point where new characters, new scenery, and a new plot had been created in the place of the normal suburban life that they had spent years creating together.

I wanted to super-glue her together. She knew what was going to come. She knew it would shatter her existence. She knew he would have no idea what he had done.

The day would come when she, too, would be replaced by a different character from his imagination. It was only a matter of time.

To this day, I don't think there is a woman in this world who would pay more money than her for a day, an hour, a minute, even a second. Time was taking her husband away from her. Bit by bit. Piece by piece. Memory by memory.

There was no way for her to buy more.

30

On the second day, God gave me two out of my three best friends.

Skylar and Hannah not only burst through the door, they practically burst through the cafeteria's wall of windows from the parking lot. They came bearing gifts, too. Makeup, princess coloring books, fruit snacks: it was like getting a care package from your mom at summer camp. They ran in screaming, and I jumped up, matching their pitch of glee as they almost tackled me onto the cafeteria table.

Everyone stared. I didn't see it because Hannah's hair was blocking my vision, but I could feel all the eyes, including the staff's, on the three way-too-happy girls who were disrupting the sea of painful heart-to-hearts and fearful conversations.

Hannah bragged about how she sped to the Fix only to get a two hundred and something dollar ticket, and that if I didn't love her forever that she would take back all the makeup she had brought me as punishment. That's when Tess turned around from her table and addressed mine.

"This guy right here could get that taken off for you, sweetheart." She was pointing at who I correctly assumed was Lawyer. After a few introductions and Tess successfully establishing the importance and high rank to my friends, she turned her back to finish the remains of her visiting hour with Lawyer.

Something wasn't right.

Stories were tumbling out of Hannah and Skylar. When their mouths couldn't keep up with the speed of their thoughts, words would get smashed together, resulting in spurts of laughter. They were waving their arms, making rude hand and facial gestures, the three of us clapping and howling like seal lions until we almost fell out of our chairs. Hannah even asked one of the nurses (luckily it was Cub) if she could have something to drink. I couldn't take her seriously as she sipped her apple juice with her pinky pointed straight to the sky which made Skylar suggest that Hannah takes her pinky and shove it elsewhere.

I looked over at Tess, amazed that she hadn't butted in on this scene of comedic opportunity.

For once, Tess sat quietly. Tears were running down her face. Lawyer looked very serious, business-like, as if he were talking to a client who he knew was guilty but was being paid out the ass to try and defend anyway. I had never seen her cry before.

That's when she flipped her chair.

The tears were gone. Tess was back but with a vengeance. She stood and hunched over Lawyer. She yelled, cursed, pointed her manicured finger at him, and made gestures wild and close enough to punch him square in the face. The whole time Lawyer just sat there unaffected, as if he had seen Tess do this a million other times at a million different venues and with a million other choice words for him.

Cub and another woman nurse escorted her out. Tess kicked and screamed as they drug her away like a prisoner of war. Once out of sight, Lawyer stood up, fixed his suit, chuckled, and walked out the doors.

On the second day, Tess's marriage fell apart in that cafeteria. Lawyer was going to lawyer up. He was tired of her "crazy antics." as Tess would recount in an overly masculine voice as her last ditch attempt to belittle her husband - soon to be ex-husband.

On the second day, I learned that money doesn't buy happiness. On the second day, I learned that power doesn't mean you're safe from harm. On the second day, I saw one of the cruelest things a human could do to another: leave when you are all they have left.

Hannah eventually had to pay her speeding ticket.

31

Day three, and May was still with us. That night, Amber had finished her smoke break and retreated inside, but I still wanted to shoot hoops. The physical activity made me feel emotions other than pain, confusion or sadness. It let me feel more solid emotions, ones I could explain. Sweat and muscle aches were all I wanted; they were simple, and I understood them. Cub, being the former athlete that he was in his prime, sympathized and let me have ten extra minutes of "outside time."

Apparently, ten minutes was all it took for May to chuck a chair at Betty who, bless her heart, just didn't have the inner voice to tell her when to stop talking. Two nurses had to restrain May and escort her into her private room. None of the Files cared where. None of the Files cared for how long. We were just glad that Hurricane May was gone.

Betty was fine; just "a tad shaking up, sugar." After about two hours, I decided that I had waited the respectable amount of time to ask one of the nurses for the details.

"So where is she?" I peeked my head over the counter while simultaneously grabbing my third Sudoku of the evening. I felt bad; this particular male nurse printed out tons of them each day, and no one did them. It wasn't until much later when I realized it was because no one else knew how.

"She's gone," he said, smiling. I couldn't tell if he was smiling because I was doing another Sudoku or because the Dark Side had gone back to its rightful place.

I cocked my head to the side, giving him my best Please-Break-It-Down-for-Me face. Being the youngest one in the Fix did have its perks after all. Maybe he thought my brain wasn't too far into the twilight zone, like Amber's, where the chances of reason or logic making an appearance are the same as the cartoon puppies on the nurse's scrubs jumping off the fabric and coming to life.

"We had to send her back home. We couldn't do anything more for her here."

Did I hear him correctly? Am I losing my marbles? She was TOO crazy, so she got to go HOME?

I could feel my cheeks heating up; they were on fucking fire. I wanted to scream. I wanted to hit. NOW I understood why they threw chairs. Why was I being held hostage while May the Monstrous got to roam free and cause destruction like God-fucking-zilla?

I sat down at the circle table in the common area - Betty to my left, Torrance across from me. They were doing those intricate adult coloring pages. Tess was watching *Naked and Afraid*. The numbers on my Sudoku weren't adding up the way I wanted them to.

I snapped the pencil.

Before Torrance or Betty could look at me, we all looked at the newcomer by the nurses' counter. He placed his bag right where I had placed Hannah's gym bag that had never seen a gym. The male nurse was tinkering with the medications in the tomb of never-ending drugs so he could distribute nighttime meds quicker. Cub must have been doing Sandra's vitals in her room because he too was out of sight.

The scruff, the beaten up gold wedding band, the flannel and faded jeans: all this made him look like a dad. He walked towards the table and sat down to my right.

Keep in mind I just demolished a pencil 12 seconds ago out of fury towards the Fix's rigged system, but my anger dissipated when he sat down. His fear was so strong I could feel it exuding off of his skin like a clammy fog.

"What's it like in here?" he whispered to me. He probably assumed that, since I was the youngest, I must've been the best bet to get a partially-sane answer. I guess he was right. At least I didn't throw chairs.

"It's okay," I said. He still wasn't convinced. I continued.

"If you brought yourself here, you must have known that you needed it, right?"

He still looked wary. That's when Cub came in from Sandra's room.

The man flipped a light switch as if having a seizure.

Within two minutes he screamed and ranted so much that Cub released him from the ward with his magical wand of a keycard.

"Why did he leave if he drove himself here?" Betty asked in genuine curiosity.

Tess, of course, responded in her typical Tess fashion.

"Well, shit! I would be freaked the fuck out too if I walked in and saw a bunch of old ladies sitting a table fucking coloring like they're six years old and drooling all over themselves."

Tess and Betty both laughed. Amber laughed, but I don't think she knew what she was laughing at. Torrance even cracked a smile. Somewhere in Tess's crude explanation, there was some truth, and they all couldn't help but laugh about it. I was the only exception.

With a broken half of my pencil in each hand, I wondered if he went home and shot himself. If he didn't have that night, what about the night after? I'll always wonder if he made it out alive.

That's one question to which I'll never get an answer.

32

Each morning a schedule was printed, highlighting the day's events. Every group therapy session and every activity neatly placed into the daily schedule was "optional" meaning if you went, it looked good on your file. The paper would show that you were improving, engaging, socializing. This meant that your ticket to get the fuck out of the Fix and back into your bed with blankets that didn't itch and pillows that eased your headache instead of contributing to it was in closer reach than if you chose to stay in your bed all day with the curtains down and the door closed.

Not all the way closed. Obviously, that wasn't allowed. Every five minutes, one of the two nurses on guard did rounds, marking what you were doing and how you felt while you were doing it. Of course, this was all up to the interpretation of the nurse. Every few hours your vitals were checked to make sure one of the Fix's doctor's hadn't written you a prescription for poison, even though that's what half of us were hoping for. No one asks how you feel unless you're in group therapy or a one-on-one session with your psychiatrist or therapist.

That's one of the main selling points of places like the Fix. The facility requires you to be seen by a therapist and a psychiatrist every day. However, Betty wasn't seen her first two days by a psychiatrist, and Tess hadn't been seen by a therapist or a psychiatrist the first week of her time spent in the Fix. I must've been one of the lucky ones because I was seen by both every day, even if I had to nag the nurses about it.

"When is my appointment? When do I see my therapist? When do I get a new prescription?"

I began to understand why everything was bulletproof. I was sent to a facility that was supposed to fix me, and here I was begging for the services I deserved and needed while my parent's insurance money was being gobbled up by the hour.

My therapist was helpful; talking things out one-on-one helped me untangle a few of the many knotted strings of my brain.

My psychiatrist was insane - even more insane than I was. He had thick round glasses and a thick German accent. He had a white beard and wore the typical white medical coat. He didn't look like a doctor. He looked like a mad scientist.

I was intrigued instantly.

I'm not saying there was not entertainment at the Fix. Some of this shit I couldn't make up if I tried, such as Tess's daily tirade, "MY HUSBAND IS GOING TO SUE YOUR ASS OFF WHEN I'M OUT OF HERE!" Or the music therapy instructor who defied expectations and actually couldn't sing a note and was then stupefied when Sandra voiced what we all were thinking. Even the art therapy girl who was no more than 24 years old, who wouldn't give us colored pencils because she feared one of us stabbing her, was nothing compared to the Tai Chi instructor that came in every other day to cleanse our auras. He helped those who attended push, pull and lean into some weird shit. Tess said he was on Ecstasy. My bet was Acid.

Looking back, I think we were both right.

My psychiatrist was fascinating over all of them. He wasn't a hippie with a guitar, or a washed up artist with crayons, or a guru that taught at the homeless shelter when he wasn't here. He was jittery and jumpy, always scribbling things down in this notebook, scribbling on his prescription pad, or scribbling his fingertips over one of the nurses' station computer keyboards. While he always had to be scribbling away with his hands, his face remained in a constant stoic state. Truth be told, I think Scribbles was more scared of us than we were of him.

Since I wasn't threatening lawsuits or trying to eat my hand off of my wrist, the tension that held up Scribble's thick-rimmed glasses eased whenever we would have our required daily meeting during my 5-day sabbatical at Casa de la Fixa.

Except for Scribbles and I never talked about my medications.

"The ones from yesterday, are they working?"

"No, sir."

"Okay, try this."

A scribble here and a scribble there and a new pill would be waiting for me at the glass window of war that I went up to three times a day.

Scribbles was unsure of how to medically treat a 21-year-old girl seeking his expertise. One time he asked me how the towels were; I said itchy. His response?

"Mine too."

He was too old, too skittish, and too dorky. Just because I was depressed didn't mean I had completely lost my sense of distasteful humor.

It was day four, and it was unknowingly my last official hangout with Scribbles. The term "appointment" was too formal for us. We liked to keep it casual which prompted me to ask him about mental illnesses casually and why he chose this line of work. Something about the love of medicine, liking to help people, and moving to Kansas tumbled out in his jumble of words. I don't know how the man did it, but he even spoke in scribbles.

I began to fade his thickly accented voice out as my mind began wondering if Tess was going to go at it again with Sandra later over the TV controller. Sandra had just ripped at Tess's hair in my imaginary Battle Royale of the Crazies when Scribbles' voice stopped my train of thought dead in its tracks.

"Wait. What did you say?" I asked, half hoping I heard him wrong and half hoping I had just bought a two dollar scratch-off and won the ultimate jackpot.

"If I had to pick a mental illness, I would be manic - constantly manic."

Scribbles' face was straight as an arrow, and I had to try to match it so I could go from the Jackpot to the Triple Jackpot Purse of Gold.

"Why is that?" I asked. To this day, how I didn't sprain a facial muscle from keeping my laughter from exploding is beyond my comprehension.

Scribbles responded with a Well-Let's-Be-Logical look on his face which almost made me want to remind him that I was a patient in a mental institution, therefore my logical credibility card was shredded when I got here.

"Being manic is amazing, Anissa. You don't sleep. You're constantly moving, doing. You never get tired. I would love to be manic," he paused and pushed his glasses up to his brow, unintentionally giving me the middle finger. "The good kind of maniac, of course."

All I could do was give a nod in agreement.

The Fix's very own psychiatrist admitted to a patient that he wishes he was manic!

Scribbles left my room, and, without a single fuck to give, I closed the door all the way, jumped on my bed, and laughed into my pillow until I cried.

I had won the Triple Jackpot Purse of Gold.

Scribbles, I hope you're reading this because you are one funny fucker.

33

My hair is longer now, especially when wet from my shower.

Two water drops descend from my clinging hair and fall down my spinal cord.

It's been ten months since my ribs were submerged in the bathtub of wine. Ten months since my toes felt the ice of the Fix's white tile floors. Ten months since Orange carelessly carted me off in a maroon van. Ten months since I met the files. Ten months since Cub woke me up. Ten months since that particular male nurse printed out a Sudoku page for me. Ten months since Scribbles wrote me my last prescription: a sturdy anti-depressant that I weaned myself off of at month nine.

The markings of frustrated swipes and uncalculated scrapes on my right forearm have faded, but my left forearm is not as fortunate. Scars mark their territory on my skin, a consistent reminder of what my demons can persuade my hands to do.

Like the pink markings of forever on my forearms, the demons have faded but still exist deep beneath the protective coverage of my skin.

Several drops fall, too many to count.

The Fix didn't fix me. The therapist didn't fix me. The prescriptions didn't fix me, although it would be a lie to say that therapists, psychiatrists, and medications that I was treated by after discharged as a File didn't help.

In a place built for crazy, I had never been saner.

Another drop.

The Fix showed me lives. It showed me, people.

It showed me Him: living proof that the body means nothing and the soul everything.

It showed me Tess and Lawyer: living proof that money means nothing and love everything.

It showed me that the world keeps turning, with or without you being an active participant.

It showed me that every life is worth living and that every life comes with a set of demons that wage inner warfare on the brain, day and night, killing and destroying everything that is set in their path.

The bathtub of wine was not the last time the demons won. My collection of scars, usually hidden by a collection of bracelets, is from inner attacks both before and after my time in the Fix.

Inner warfare doesn't stop, but that doesn't mean you can't win.

Water rests on the shower's porcelain edges. Water invisibly covers the white tile of my bathroom where my undried feet have marked their path. Water falls from the split ends of my wet hair and trickles down the small of my back, sending chills through my shoulders, down to my arms, to the finish line of my typing fingers.

Chills that prove I am living proof.

Living.

I am not ending with blood.

I am ending with water.

Made in the USA
Monee, IL
03 January 2020